'The w … people are ask … s book Dave F … elevant topics for young people today and helps them see the good news, that God has a plan and it is good.'

ALISTAIR CHALMERS, author of *Road Map to Jesus*

'*What You Are Made For* is culturally relevant, with specific, real-world help for young adults who are seeking their purpose in life. Dave keeps his balance perfectly on the tricky path between our individuality and our call to live in community, showing that our uniqueness is how we serve.'

H.R. HESS, author of the Callenlas Chronicles

'*What You Are Made For* offers teenagers an engaging blend of practical tools and biblical wisdom as they seek answers to the questions we all have about our life's purpose and meaning.'

CASSIE MARTIN, author of *Genuine*

'An accessible book that empowers and encourages as it takes you on a journey of discovering your purpose.'

MILLIE, Aged 16

YOUR GUIDE TO FINDING PURPOSE

WHAT YOU ARE MADE FOR

DAVE BODEN

10 Publishing
a division of 10 of those.com

British Library Cataloguing in Publication Data
A record for this book is available from the British Library

ISBN: 9781837280339
Designed by Jude May
Cover image © greyj | iStock

Printed in Denmark
10Publishing, a division of 10ofthose.com
Unit C, Tomlinson Road, Leyland, PR25 2DY, England
info@10ofthose.com
www.10ofthose.com

1 3 5 7 10 8 6 4 2

This book is dedicated to my children Nyah, Joel, Micah, and Sienna.

May you find your purpose the way God helped me find mine.

CONTENTS

INTRO 9

CHAPTER 1: FINDING YOUR THING 13

CHAPTER 2: TALENTS 27

CHAPTER 3: HOPES 43

CHAPTER 4: INFLUENCES 61

CHAPTER 5: NEGATIVES 79

CHAPTER 6: GROWTH 97

OUTRO 117

INTRO

They say the two most important days in your life are the day you're born and the day you discover why. You're here on planet earth for a reason, and this book is designed to help you unlock this purpose.

It's worth knowing from the get-go that we focus on a Christian perspective throughout this book. *What You Are Made For* is based on ancient wisdom that has been around for thousands of years, and it can totally transform your life.

At the heart of Christianity is the most famous person in all of history – Jesus. If you aren't quite sure who he is, why he came, and why that would even matter to a young person like yourself, you could check out my first book *Like or Follow: What Every Teenager Needs to Decide about Jesus.*

Curious about what comes next once you're a Christian? Read on.

Each short chapter explores an aspect of how you can live purposefully. We start with a sentence that sums up the point in a nutshell and at the end of each chapter there are questions to reflect on either by yourself or with someone you trust. We'll think about how and why God has made and shaped you; what influences will help or hinder you; and how to overcome barriers to living out what you are made for.

HIGHLIGHT REEL: DAVID'S STORY

Throughout this book, we'll be digging into the Bible. Whenever you see a quote like this:

> The LORD will fulfil his purpose for me; your steadfast love, O LORD, endures forever. (Psalm 138:8, ESV)

...the name and number refer to the part of the Bible the quote comes from. Need to know how to find a Bible verse? Psalms 138:8 = the Bible book 'Psalms', chapter 138 (the big numbers in each Bible book) and verse 8 (the small numbers in each chapter). The letters (like 'ESV') let you know which translation of the Bible has been used. If there are no letters, the quote comes from the New International Version.

You'll also discover insights from the life of David, in the Old Testament, through 'highlight reels' like this one. David wrote the words quoted above.

David was a young shepherd boy who became one of the greatest kings of ancient Israel after his humble start in life. He famously defeated the giant Goliath with just a sling and a stone. Though he was a musician and poet who wrote many of the psalms in the Bible, his life wasn't always easy. He faced betrayal, emotional struggles, and made big mistakes, but always turned back to God. Through it all, the life of David reminds us that God can use anyone, no matter their issues, to fulfil his purpose.

You can read David's life story in the Bible beginning at 1 Samuel 16 and continuing through to 1 Kings 2. Exploring David's journey can help you find your own purpose. Along the way, David reminds us that Jesus is our ultimate example – showing us the best way to live, love, and fulfil our destiny.

Here's the good news: God had a purpose for this world long before you tried to figure out your own. This means instead of stressing about finding your own way, life is about getting on board with what God is already up to.

Have you ever played that crazy video game *Just Dance?* It's all about copying the moves you see on the screen to rack up points, level up, and outshine the competition. The more you dance, the tougher it gets, and eventually, you're barely keeping up. It's exhausting trying to nail every move perfectly!

But finding God's purpose for your life isn't like that. It's not about meeting a very narrow set of criteria to qualify or following a complicated set of rules. You don't need to worry about getting everything exactly right or feel pressured to plan out the next twenty or thirty years of your life. Living purposefully starts right where you are. It's about growing, learning, and discovering how to be a part of what God is doing in the world, one step at a time. This book will show you how to make the first move.

CHAPTER 1

FINDING YOUR THING

WHY AM I HERE?

YOU WERE MADE FOR A PURPOSE.

Nobody thought a movie about a plastic doll would make over a billion dollars at the box office, but guess what? *Barbie* smashed it and became a massive global sensation. Perhaps you were there on the opening weekend decked out in your best pink feather boa and a cowboy hat. Alternatively, maybe you'd rather watch paint dry on a TikTok livestream than even sit through the 3-minute trailer but, either way, for a while *Barbie* was everywhere.

The film featured this powerful song, 'What Was I Made For?' by Billie Eilish. The lyrics hit way deeper than you'd expect for a comedy.

In the music video, Billie Eilish sits at a classroom desk, popping open a vintage trunk full of mini versions of iconic outfits from her career – think tiny Gucci tracksuits, Chanel Oscars outfits, and even a yellow jumpsuit, all ready to be set up on a mini rack.

Out of nowhere, the ground starts shaking, the wind's howling, and rain is coming down hard while Billie's hustling to set up her wardrobe amidst the chaos. She's freaked out, trying to stay in control and keep the show rolling but she knows ultimately she can't. Who is she really?

When the rain finally stops, Billie gives up, shoving all the soaked outfits back in the trunk. She disappears off screen, leaving the table and chairs empty. Then it hits us – maybe this isn't just your average music video? It's a lesson about how, when everything feels like it's crumbling, we long for purpose. We want to know what we are made for.

Billie Eilish isn't the only one asking the question. People have been trying to figure out their purpose for centuries.

Over 2,400 years ago, the famous philosopher Aristotle claimed that 'Happiness is the meaning and the purpose of life.' Although lots of people think that today too, this answer hasn't worked in practice. After all, feelings can go up and down, like a rollercoaster. What if you have a bad day? Or what if something that makes me happy hurts someone else? Aren't some things important to do even if they're hard? Surely we were made for something better than just feeling good?

Of course, asking 'What was I made for?' implies that you were made for a reason. Not everyone believes this is true. Some people say we're all just random accidents of nature. Maybe we're just a bunch of molecules that somehow got zapped into life after millions of years of evolution? Maybe there's no big plan and we might as well just try and make the best of things?

As Christians we know that there is more to life than this. Right from the very start of the Bible we discover God is a creator who made everything for a purpose.

> Then the LORD God formed a man from the dust of the ground and breathed into his nostrils the breath of life, and the man became a living being. (Genesis 2:7)

You and I are not just here by accident. Just like everything else created has a purpose, so do we. A guitar is designed to play music. A pen to write. A watch to tell the time. So what about us? What are *we* made for?

DISCOVERING WHAT MATTERS

Let's imagine for a moment that a big green alien comes to visit planet earth with a mission to learn about the purpose of humankind. We'll call our alien Bob. Bob the Alien spends a week seeing movies, binge-watching TV shows, scrolling through social media, and listening to pop songs. After one week on earth, Bob returns to his home planet and reports back to all the other aliens on what he has found.

According to the media, humans are made:

- To hustle for success.
- To be better than the rest.
- To chase after fame.
- To be entertained.
- To keep buying stuff.
- To conform and fit in.
- To find their perfect match and fall in love.
- To rack up those likes and hearts on social media.
- To feel good all the time.
- To find answers in themselves.

Aliens may not be real, but the media messages are. Feeding on a diet that fills your mind and heart with this kind of stuff is enough to make anyone feel burnt out. It's no wonder so many teens feel anxious, depressed, and like their life is never going to amount to anything. While the media shouts this rubbish at us every single day, this is totally alien (excuse the pun) to how the Bible describes God's purpose for our lives.

YOU WERE MADE TO BELONG!

In the Bible, we get a sneak peek into why God

planned to make humans in the first place. He wasn't just bored and fancied a bit of an experiment. He didn't need some mindless minions to boss around. His world isn't some video game to keep himself amused full of human NPCs – non-playable characters. Instead, he wanted to build a family. Incredibly, when we decide to follow Jesus we can know that we belong to him:

> Long before he laid down earth's foundations, he [God] had us in mind, had settled on us as the focus of his love, to be made whole and holy by his love. Long, long ago he decided to adopt us into his family through Jesus Christ. (What pleasure he took in planning this!) (Ephesians 1:4–5, MSG)

YOU WERE MADE TO BE LOVED!

God loves people more than anything else in all his creation. People are his MVPs – most valuable players. His heart for the world is huge: he wants everyone on the planet to experience his love. No one is ever seen as a minion by God. And when we turn to him and accept this love we can be sure we will always be his child.

Becoming part of God's family matters more than anything else. It's the foundation for everything we do. The amazing thing about this is that we are accepted into God's family – not because we are good enough – but because of how good God is. All we need to do is trust in Jesus to rescue us from our sins and turn to him, knowing God loves us no matter what. This changes everything! When we know we're loved and that we belong, we can start to figure out our own place in the world and what God's plan for us might be.

DISCOVERING YOUR THING

The Disney-Pixar movie *Soul* follows the story of Joe Gardner. He's a jazz musician who, just as he gets his big break in life, has a freak accident and ends up in a heaven-like place called the 'Great Before'. There, Joe meets 22, a quirky small greenish-blue transparent blob of a soul who hasn't found her purpose yet. During the film they have many conversations about the meaning of life and 22 is worried she won't figure hers out. At one point 22 exclaims:

> 'They say you're born to do something, but how do you figure out what that thing is?

> And what if you pick up the wrong thing? Or somebody else's thing, you know? Then you're stuck!'

It might sound like an amazing idea to live out our God-given purpose, but how do we get on and choose what to do? There's a whole lot of options out there, what if we pick the wrong thing? What if we make a mistake and end up doing someone else's thing? Most Disney movies tend to conclude that we can find the answers within ourselves. If we 'look within' to try and discover our meaning, we'll probably always feel worried we've missed our true purpose. Trying to figure out our purpose solely by looking within ourselves is like trying to understand how to work a complex machine without an instruction manual – you need to consult the maker to figure out what it is made for. You need something or someone beyond yourself.

The key to finding your purpose is realising that God had one long before you ever did. When we centre our lives on God, his priorities and purposes become ours too. He's in the business of loving people by saving them and bringing them into his family. Jesus came as the ultimate expression of God's love for us. Just like the most famous verse in the Bible says:

> For this is how God loved the world: He gave his one and only Son, so that everyone who believes in him will not perish but have eternal life. (John 3:16, NLT)

Remember we were made to be loved and to belong! To find our purpose, we trust in Jesus to reconnect us to God. And then we spend the rest of our lives following Jesus and getting on board with his plans! By following Jesus, we learn how to love the world the way God does.

Jesus shares a big secret about what the focus of our life ought to be. It's found in Matthew 22:37–39 in the Bible:

> 'Love the Lord your God with all your heart and with all your soul and with all your mind.' This is the first and greatest commandment. And a second is like it: 'Love your neighbour as yourself.'

These two instructions are at the heart of everything we'll talk about in this book. If you're trying to figure out what you were born for, start by thinking about how you can love God and love the people around you. That's the foundation for discovering your purpose.

Loving God is our response to his character, actions, and constant presence through life's ups and downs. He offers us a love that never ends, never fails, and is deeply personal, which naturally makes us want to love him back. It's like falling in love with someone – the more you get to know them, the more you want them in your life. And when we experience God's love for us, we want to pass on this same love to those around us.

When you live by these two commands – loving God and loving others – you're living out the purpose God has for your life. It's about putting love at the centre of everything you do.

WHERE TO START?

We're all called to get on board with God's plans in the world but this will look slightly different for each of us.

Here are five questions you can ask yourself (based on an acronym of the word T.H.I.N.G.) to help discover exactly what loving God and others means for you in your day-to-day life:

T is for Talents: What are my God-given talents?
H is for Hopes: What do I hope and dream for?
I is for Influences: Who or what influences me most?
N is for Negatives: What challenges do I need to overcome?
G is for Growth: How do I grow in my purpose?

When you start to figure these questions out, it can almost feel like unlocking a superpower!

It's easy to think that God's purpose for you is something way off in the future, but the truth is, you can start right now. You don't need to hop on a plane or travel to the other side of the world to begin. Start where you are. You don't need a special qualification or to join a secret club. Start with who you are.

As Christians worldwide listened to Billie Eilish's 'What Was I Made For?', young people responded with creativity, expressing the purpose they found through Jesus. Many began rewriting the song's lyrics, infusing them with faith-filled messages to share their belief in Christ's vision for their lives.

One creator, Martay, took the song and turned it into a worship version. The lyrics talk about how she felt relieved after realising she doesn't have to fit in with everyone else. Instead, she found out that her real purpose is to live for God, not to meet other people's expectations.[1]

You can learn to live with this kind of confidence, too. In a world that feels like it is constantly changing and shaking all around us, the good news is that we can know who we are and why we were born.

You weren't created to find your worth in social media likes. You weren't designed to just hustle for success, outdo others, or follow the crowd. You weren't meant to chase fame, seek constant entertainment, or just keep buying stuff.

You were made for a purpose.

QUESTIONS TO THINK ABOUT: WHY AM I HERE?

- Why do you think it is often hard to figure out your purpose in life?
- What might be the benefits of discovering your thing?
- How does Jesus' teaching to 'love God' and 'love others' help us find our purpose?

CHAPTER 2

TALENTS

WHAT ARE MY GOD-GIVEN TALENTS?

YOU WERE MADE TO MAKE A DIFFERENCE.

When most people hear the word 'talent' they automatically think about *Britain's Got Talent* or *America's Got Talent*. These insanely popular shows certainly attract a particular set of skills!

Take the Regurgitator, for example, with his disgusting ability to swallow and then spit back up various objects, including live goldfish, silver coins, and billiard balls. DO NOT TRY THIS AT HOME! Or my personal favourite Jokgu, the piano-playing chicken – an actual chicken who made it through the first auditions with her amazing keyboard skills. But sadly, her second shot didn't go as well. Jokgu and her sister were supposed to peck out the tune 'Born to be Wild', but they totally froze on stage. I guess she got cold (clawed) feet.

Training chickens or swallowing stuff might not be your thing, but we all have talents. Talents are simply the things we're good at. They are the strengths and skills you're born with that sometimes you don't even notice until you face a new experience or challenge that brings one out.

If I were to ask you a question like, 'What are you *not* good at?', I'm guessing you could immediately give me a long list of all the things you don't get right. You might hear your friends say stuff like 'I'm not smart enough here', or 'I could do better in that'. Ask someone what they are good at, on the other hand, and they tend to go silent fast. It feels a lot harder to identify our strengths, let alone talk about them. But the truth is God has made everyone with things they are good at and he wants us to use these talents to love others!

In this chapter, we'll explore how discovering our talents can guide us towards what we should be doing in life. But it's important to remember that talents alone aren't the whole story. It's easy to get caught up in the idea that you need to excel at something to prove your worth. But, as we saw in chapter 1, we are created to belong to God and be part of his family. Your talents don't make you special; God does.

In the Christian faith, you're not judged by being the best at something like in a variety show. God is not like Simon Cowell waiting to press his buzzer when you don't perform well enough. You don't have to be a piano-playing chicken to impress your creator!

Unlike some of the crazy self-centred attention seeking escapades you see in a talent show, we are encouraged to take our eyes off ourselves and start putting others first. It's not all about you. Instead we should be sharing our gifts, talents, time, and resources for the benefit of those around us.

The Bible sums this up in one simple sentence:

> Each of you should use whatever gift you have received to serve others... (1 Peter 4:10)

Our talents are not given just to express our own creativity, help us take centre stage, win the approval of others, or seek fame and fortune. They are wonderfully designed to show God's heart to the world. God's all about loving people, and your talents are meant to do the same. That could mean showing people who Jesus is, making a difference in the world around you, or choosing to serve others instead of just focusing on yourself.

'But how do I know what my talents are?', you might ask. It's not always easy to 'talent spot' yourself.

YOU ARE CRAFTED

Ever tried one of those personality tests, to discover which emoji, or classic video game character, or princess you are? These quizzes are not exactly scientific and more likely designed to show you more ads and collect your phone data. (I'm always Princess Belle, apparently!)

There are better ways to figure out what you are skilled at. Unpacking a list of every single talent would be endless, but you can start pinpointing your own by thinking in terms of how you are CRAFTED.

Look through the CRAFTED Framework and pick out the two or three that relate most to you:

C – Creative *Artistic Talents*	These are talents related to expressing creativity, like drawing, painting, making music, writing stories or poems, acting in plays or making YouTube videos – anything that lets you show your imagination and feelings through art.
R – Resourceful *Practical Talents*	These are talents related to hands-on work and fixing things, like building stuff, DIY projects, repairing things, gardening, and working out solutions to practical problems.

A – Academic *Intellectual Talents*	These are talents related to learning and thinking, like solving problems, researching topics, understanding how things work, tackling equations, and processing information.
F – Friendly *Social Talents*	These are talents related to connecting with others, like listening well, understanding others' feelings, making friends with lots of different types of people, working well in teams, and helping others when they need it.
T – Technical *Professional Talents*	These are talents related to working, organising, and administering things well, managing big projects, and using specialist technology like creating websites, apps, or coding.

E – Empowering *Leadership Talents*	These are talents related to leading and motivating others, like teaching, speaking in front of groups, inspiring people, solving problems together, teamwork, and being a positive influence on others.
D – Dynamic *Physical Talents*	These are talents related to being active, like playing sports, staying fit, dancing, enjoying outdoor activities, and participating in physical challenges that require strength, coordination, and movement.

The CRAFTED Framework is a way to group different types of skills together so you can think clearly about who you are. You may say, 'Well, I'm a bit of this but *a lot* of that.' And that's the point. You will probably relate more to some types of talents than others. One talent is not better than another – they are just different. Remember, you never have to compare yourself to someone else.

YOU ARE UNIQUE

The CRAFTED Framework shows how each person is naturally gifted at different things. God made each of us as unique as a fingerprint, a personal signature, or a one-of-a-kind painting. It is the unique blend of our gifts, talents, and personality that make us who we are.

> For you created my inmost being; you knit me together in my mother's womb. I praise you because I am fearfully and wonderfully made; your works are wonderful, I know that full well. (Psalm 139:13–14)

Think about how these young people fit into the CRAFTED Framework.

Shay is the ultimate brainiac, always acing exams like it's no big deal. She's all about science, chess, and academic challenges. But Shay also loves being active, playing rugby, swimming, and boxing. Plus, she's got a heart for helping others, using her social talents to mentor younger students and share her faith with her teammates. Shay is *Academic, Dynamic,* and *Friendly*.

Ben is always building computers from scratch or fixing up bikes. He's forever solving practical problems. He's also a tech whiz, coding simple games and managing his church's youth website. Beyond that, Ben's leadership talents shine as he runs a club that teaches others how to build and code. Ben is *Resourceful, Technical,* and *Empowering.*

Lila is the creative spirit of her friendship group, always sketching, painting, or writing stories. She brings her artistic talents to life in drama class, where she acts in school plays. But Lila is also a caring friend who's great at understanding others and offering support. Lila is *Creative* and *Friendly.*

Now, what about you? How might the CRAFTED Framework help describe who you are?

HIGHLIGHT REEL: DAVID'S TALENTS

The Bible is full of characters who God used in amazing ways even when they were far from perfect. Take David for example. If we compare him against the CRAFTED Framework, you can see his talents shining through. David was *Resourceful* as a hands-on shepherd. Yet he was also an *Empowering* leader – as king he shaped the whole nation of Israel to love and serve God. Perhaps one of his most impactful talents though was his creativity.

David's *Creative* talents were a big part of how he worshipped God and helped others to do the same. He was a musician and songwriter, and he didn't just keep those skills to himself. When King Saul was distressed, David played his harp, and it helped bring him peace. That's how powerful music can be. You can read about this in 1 Samuel 16:14–23.

David's songs are full of raw emotion and a deliberate focus on God. Some are psalms of praise, others a cry to God for help or comfort. His songs form part of the Bible, and they've been helping people connect with God for generations. Imagine writing song lyrics that would still be read thousands of years later! His creativity wasn't just a hobby to keep him amused on quiet evenings – it was a way of connecting to his Father in a deep, real way. He showed music and writing aren't just things to pass the time – they can actually inspire others and encourage their faith, bringing people closer to God.

So, if you've got creative talents – whether it's making music, drawing, or creating YouTube videos – don't underestimate what God can do with those gifts. David's life shows that creativity, like all the other talent-types, can point people to something bigger than ourselves.

YOU ARE ABLE

If you are still struggling to identify what your talents are, then here are five top tips to help you figure things out.

- **TIP 1:** *Reflect on yourself.* Think about what you enjoy doing the most in your free time. What we do when we get a choice says a lot about us. What do you always talk passionately about? What makes you feel alive? Do you ever start something and totally lose track of time? That's a sign you are doing what comes naturally!

- **TIP 2:** *Think backwards.* What did you always end up doing as a little kid when you had the chance? What were you known for when you were younger? What did you win and succeed at early on? What have you always been excited about?

- **TIP 3:** *Ask others.* Your family, friends, teachers, and your church youth leaders, will happily point out some of your strengths. Ask five people and then make a list! It may even be good to ask a few people who are new in your life to give you their positive first impressions.

- **TIP 4:** *Consider what frustrates you.* Your gift is sometimes hidden behind what makes you annoyed. You might always help others sort out or fix something that is plain and obvious to you but is hard for them. It may even frustrate you that people don't see things the same as you. The way you want to help others can be a hint about who you are.

- **TIP 5:** *Challenge yourself.* Do something outside of your comfort zone. When you put yourself in a new situation, it unlocks new strengths that you never knew you had. Ask people around you at home and church – what needs doing? Then give that thing a try!

If the purpose of God for our lives is to love him and love people then there is no better way to start than by using our talents for the benefit of others. But this is not just about us as individuals. One of the reasons why being part of a church community is so valuable is that we get to work together, pooling our gifts and talents, to serve God by serving those around us. Together we are always stronger. The Bible describes this as like being part of a body.

> Just as our bodies have many parts and each part has a special function, so it is with Christ's body. We are many parts of one body, and we all belong to each other. (Romans 12:4–5, NLT)

Just like a body has different parts – like hands, feet, and eyes – each of us has our own special role to play. Nobody needs to act like someone they are not or try to be the same as everyone else. Imagine a body made up of just massive feet. Gross! Or think of a body made of just a giant eye (like Mike in *Monsters, Inc.*)! It just wouldn't work.

Each part is crucial for the body to function properly. If one part isn't doing its job, the whole body struggles. Just as every body part works together to keep the body healthy and active, everyone's gifts work together to support and strengthen God's church and reach out to others. That's why we need other Christians and they need us!

You were made to make a difference.

QUESTIONS TO THINK ABOUT:
WHAT ARE MY GOD-GIVEN TALENTS?

- Which talents relate most to you in the 'CRAFTED Framework'?
- What could you do today to better develop your talents?
- How can you use your talents to make a difference?

CHAPTER 3

HOPES

WHAT DO I HOPE AND DREAM FOR?

YOU WERE MADE TO SHARE GOD'S HOPE WITH THE WORLD.

Fans of *The Simpsons* are convinced the show has predicted the future better than real-life experts ever since it first aired in 1989. From the winner of the 2016 American Presidential Election, to Lady Gaga hosting the Super Bowl, and even the shape of The Shard in London before it was built, *The Simpsons* has a crazy track record of eerily accurate predictions. It has also imagined tech like smartwatches, FaceTime, autocorrect text messages, and even the Apple Vision Pro way before its time!

Unfortunately, when it comes to our real lives, we find it much harder than Homer Simpson to predict what's coming next. Some picture their future as gloomy, while others see it shining with endless possibilities. The difference between seeing things as positive or negative comes down to one small word: hope.

Living without hope is a terrible thing. It leaves you feeling unmotivated, stuck in negative thoughts, and like you have no meaning. And even when we have hope, we can end up disappointed if the something or someone we've put our hope in lets us down.

Everyone attaches their hope to something.

- 'I hope that my football team will win.'
- 'I hope I win the lottery.'
- 'I hope I make friends in my new school.'
- 'I hope I get my dream job.'

Some hope in their own abilities, thinking they can bet on themselves for a better future. Some trust in politicians, world leaders, or even celebrities to make the world better. Others spend their whole lives hoping for that perfect romantic relationship to come along and fulfil their wildest dreams.

For Christians, our ultimate hope is found in God. The Bible backs the idea that God offers the kind of hope that is better than what you will find anywhere else. Romans 15:13 says:

> May the God of hope fill you with all joy and peace as you trust in him, so that you may overflow with hope...

This is a reminder that Christians are called to be the most hopeful people in the world. Why? Because they put their hope in God's plan not their own.

Even when things feel hard or confusing, we know they aren't spinning out of control. God reassures us that his love for us remains secure at all times. Hope is about knowing that your life and future have meaning and purpose, no matter what you're going through right now. Hope isn't just about wishing things will get better – it's trusting that God has a plan for your life, and he is working out everything for your good to help you become more like Jesus.

And when we know this, we can start to dream.

OUR HOPE GIVES US VISION

A vision is about having a clear idea of what you want your future to look like. It means setting a goal or developing a dream that gives you direction and motivation. Vision helps you figure out what you're aiming for in life, whether it's who you want to become, what you want to achieve, or how you want to make a difference. When you start to dream, you're allowing time to explore the gifts and passions God has placed within you. For example, you might be drawn to using your talents in music to lead worship or feel a strong pull to help others through mission work. These dreams give you a glimpse into how God might be guiding you.

Without a vision for the future, people tend to live by accident.

In Disney's original, animated *Alice in Wonderland*, there's a scene where Alice finds herself lost in the woods. Unsure of where to go, she asks the Cheshire Cat for directions. The cat responds with a question: 'Where do you want to get to?'

When Alice admits she doesn't really know, the cat famously says, 'Then it really doesn't matter which way you go.' This highlights the problem for so many of us. We have no sense of direction, so we don't know which way to go. We're left feeling lost.

But here's why there is always good news with Jesus: God has a plan for this world that is far bigger and better than we can imagine, and each of us has a role in it! For anyone – young people included – feeling lost or unsure of their path, God's plan offers a clear direction. Unlike Alice, who doesn't know where to go, you don't have to wander hopelessly around.

God has given us the best news ever. He sent Jesus, his Son, to fix things up for us. Jesus showed us how to love and be kind to one another. But more than that, he was crucified on the cross, taking on all the bad stuff we've done. He died to sort out our mess and bring us into God's family. But wait for it – three days later, he's back from the dead, proving no matter how dark it gets, God is still working out his plan. We have hope because Jesus proved he's stronger than any evil on earth.

When Christ came to earth he gave us a new vision of hope for the whole world. This vision helps us imagine a better future because of what Jesus has done for us. This is why Christians can find hope even in difficult times; they still live in a world full of mess, but they know this is not how things will be forever.

Sometimes our personal goals can distract us from God's plan if they are only centred on ourselves. Jesus offers a better way to filter our life goals to make sure they fit into God's bigger vision for the world.

We saw back in chapter 1 that Jesus taught our number one priority in life is to love God with everything we have – our hearts and minds and soul and strength. This is known as 'the Great Commandment'. Our number two priority flows straight from the first – we should love our neighbours (anyone!) as we love ourselves. So loving God involves loving other people and taking care of them in the same way we would like to be treated.

If you've ever gone off course on a journey, you know that a Sat Nav will always get you back on track. The Great Commandment is like our Sat Nav for life, showing us the best route to follow. It can reorient you back to the right path when you feel like you've gone in the wrong direction. No matter how far you've drifted, the Great Commandment will always recalculate and redirect. So, how do I know if my vision is in line with God's plan? Simply ask yourself: Do my plans help me love God and love other people better? If that's the case, then go for it! Love is the secret ingredient to any God-fuelled vision.

OUR HOPE MOVES US TO ACTION

As young teenagers, brothers Alex and Brett Harris caught hold of a hopeful vision that inspired them to start a movement in the USA called 'The Rebelution' which has gone on to make an impact all over the world. They firmly believe that young people don't have to wait till they're older to start creating a better world. Here is an extract from their vision for all young people:

> 'We are a teenage rebellion against low-expectations. When culture tells us we don't

> have anything to offer until we've drained our teen years wasting our "meaningless" time on ourselves, *we beg to differ*. We believe God has given us the gifts, talents, time, and energy to enter the fray of world-changers and start bringing God's kingdom to earth "as it is in heaven." Whether that's serving our church, starting a kids club in our neighbourhood, writing a book, starting a non-profit [a charity], or simply taking our little brother out for ice-cream – we're ready to step into the opportunities God has laid right in front of us.'[2]

This is an inspiring call to action, reminding us that God's purpose isn't just for the future – it's for all young people right now. The great thing about living a hope-fuelled life is that you don't have to drop out of school or quit your job to do it. Each of us can get stuck in right where we are.

You can live out your own version of a 'Loving God and Loving Others' mission.

This is where the CRAFTED Framework from the previous chapter helps us see how our different talents help us to share God's hope with others.

Creative:	A person with *Artistic Talents* might envision sharing God's truth through inspiring art and multimedia.
Resourceful:	Someone with *Practical Talents* could have a long-term vision of building houses for those trapped in poverty but start by raising money for a local charity by upcycling old furniture.
Academic:	An individual with *Intellectual Talents* might aspire to start a blog series that explores complex topics in a way that educates their generation about the Christian faith.
Friendly:	A person gifted with *Social Talents* might seek to organise community gatherings where people can come together to feel like they belong.
Technical:	Teenagers with *Professional Talents* could help organise events or coordinate volunteers to serve those in need.
Empowering:	Young people with *Leadership Talents* might dream of pioneering new ways of changing their school, college or work place for the better.
Dynamic:	Those with *Physical Talents* might pursue sports in a way that displays God's character through their loving attitude to others and spirit of excellence.

Want to get started? Simply answer the question 'Who is my neighbour and how can I show them love?' Then think about the skills you have, the passion in your heart, and start to share your hope with others. This may look like:

- A teen studying health and social care could volunteer at an old people's home, offering care to those who need it most. That might bring hope to our neighbours who are elderly.
- An aspiring teacher could mentor younger children, guiding them to discover their own talents. That might bring hope to our neighbours who are young.
- Teenagers interested in business could start something that's fair, ethical, and gives back to the community. That might bring hope to our neighbours who are poor.
- Young authors could write stories that lift people up; sharing messages of faith, hope, and love with their peers. That might bring hope to our neighbours who are online.

You can see how all of these 'little missions' are unique like you and me, but they all fit into that 'love God' and 'love others' criteria. The list could go on and on. The possibilities are endless for those that choose to live with hope.

Whether we're at school, home, with friends, or even hanging out online, God calls each of us to make a difference for him right where we are. These are the places where we spend most of our time every day, and because of who we are in Christ, God can use us to bring hope to others.

Individually, this works great, but when we come together as the church, something powerful happens. You can team up with others to tackle social justice issues, meet more community needs, and reach out to different types of people in new and exciting ways. This is why being part of a church community offers so many chances to help make a real impact for others.

HIGHLIGHT REEL: DAVID'S VISION

David had a hope and a dream to build a temple that would be a permanent home for God's people to worship God. We first hear him sharing this dream with a man called Nathan in 2 Samuel 7. Later he gathered materials, made detailed plans, and organised the workers and resources needed in preparation for his vision to become reality.

However, in the end, David himself wouldn't be the one to carry out these plans because God meant for his son Solomon to build the temple. David was able to pass on his dream to the next generation.

David's dream of building a temple for God was about creating something lasting and meaningful – a place where people could connect with God for generations. It's a great reminder for young people today who have a vision or goal for the future. Even if you don't get to see it all happen yourself, what you start can still inspire others. Live with hope and others catch it.

David's vision pointed to something even bigger to come in Jesus. The temple David dreamed of was a place where people could worship God, but Jesus offers us something even better – a personal relationship with God that isn't limited to any one place. We no longer have to go to a physical building to meet with God, we just have to go to Jesus. The good news is that through Jesus, we have access to God anytime, anywhere.

OUR HOPE CAN BE CONTAGIOUS

The Secret Millionaire was a TV show that featured the super-rich going undercover in communities trapped by poverty, volunteering in a local charity to learn more about the problems faced by people there. At the end of the show, they revealed their identity and donated money, which transformed the lives of those involved. Whenever the millionaires met people in hopeless circumstances, they already knew they had the financial means to turn things around. This gave them a totally different perspective on the problems in front of them.

We probably don't have a million quid to give away, nor do we put our faith in our own ability to fix everything, but we can have a positive perspective because we carry God's hope with us every day. We can walk into situations that seem lost, broken, and a total mess, and see them differently because we know what Jesus can do.

We can live with hope for the future, knowing that one day, there will be no more pain, sadness, or injustice anymore. One day, Jesus will return and fix everything. It will be heaven – or what is known as 'the new creation'.

- In the new creation people will find freedom from poverty.
- In the new creation no one will go hungry.
- In the new creation the sick will be made forever well.
- In the new creation Jesus will put an end to all conflict and there will be perfect peace.

It will be heaven on earth. This is our hope!

And if that's not exciting enough: Jesus promised that he's bringing real change to the world right now, and he's doing it through us – his people. Throughout history, Christians have helped people out of poverty and hunger, and worked for peace and healing. They've brought God's hope to desperate situations. This is good news!

Sharing this good news is as simple as talking to your friends about what God has done in your life. You could tell them how he helps you through tough times, gives you peace when you're stressed, or gives you purpose when you feel lost. It's not about preaching, but just being real with people about your faith and showing them how Jesus can make a difference in their lives, too.

By living with hope and joy, others will notice something different in you, and that's when you can share the reason for your hope – God's love through Jesus. Whether it's through your actions, words, or just being there for someone, you're showing them that there's a bigger story at play, and that no matter what, God's love and hope are available to them.

Why don't you ask God to show you something hopeful in the midst of a hopeless world? There may be specific things that God gives you a vision for, which end up defining how you live your life. So, will you dare to dream?

At the end of the day, there are two ways we can live. We can live as if there is no hope and no purpose; we can act as if things are only going to get worse. Or we can believe that God has a purpose for his world, and we can live with his hope in our hearts now.

We can live like we have seen the end of the movie, and we already know that everything will work out in the end. We can live knowing Jesus has already won the victory.

You were made to share God's hope with the world.

QUESTIONS TO THINK ABOUT: WHAT DO I HOPE AND DREAM FOR?

- Why do you think Jesus is such good news in our hopeless world?
- What do you hope for in the lives of those around you?
- How might you start to share your hope with others?

CHAPTER 4

INFLUENCES

WHO OR WHAT INFLUENCES ME MOST?

YOU WERE MADE TO FOLLOW JESUS.

When YouTubers Logan Paul and KSI dropped a bombshell announcement that they were launching a line of energy drinks called Prime, the hype was immediate with their 40 million followers buzzing about it online.

The taste? Pretty average, really. But that didn't stop people going nuts for it.

Prime sold out almost immediately after launch, and bottles would resell for up to £400 for a pack of twelve online. Newspapers reported scenes of total chaos at local supermarkets as teenagers rushed to buy new bottles as soon as they came back in stock. Blue Raspberry, Ice Pop, Meta Moon... Bedrooms were full of wall to wall displays of empty bottles.

School teachers retold stories about students who, upon buying one of the brightly coloured bottles with 'PRIME' written in big, bold letters, instantly became popular and attained fame amongst their peers. Some schools banned it because of the high caffeine content, which only made it more popular.

This is the power of social influencers.

Miquela Sousa, a Brazilian-American Instagram star, better known as Lil Miquela, has over 3 million followers and has been named one of Time Magazine's '25 Most Influential People on the Internet'. She earns millions from her own clothing line and regularly collaborates with brands such as Prada, BMW, and Timberland, as well as topping the charts with her indie music.

Miquela regularly posts online, asking her audience questions like, 'Should I keep my hair like this?' or she'll post a holiday pic next to a national landmark and say, 'I wonder if I'll be around as long as this monument?'

But here's the twist: she's not real.

Lil Miquela is a virtual influencer designed by artificial intelligence. Yet her millions of followers (AKA 'Miqaliens') still choose to follow her, copying her opinions, and imitating her style. Some are even jealous of her life even though they know she's not real!

Real or fake, influencers advertise stuff while promising to help you become a better version of yourself (even though they have no idea who you really are). When they share an opinion or hot take, suddenly everyone parrots out the same ideas. And this is where it becomes serious. People alter the course of their lives based on what influencers say.

In this chapter we will discover how different types of influences can help or hinder you living out your purpose.

INFLUENCED BY OTHERS

Marcus Rashford isn't just a fantastic football player – he's a role model for young people worldwide. He's gained a huge fan base not just for his amazing skills on the field, but also for the positive things he does off it. Rashford uses his fame to speak up for social justice and equality, driven by his Christian faith. His campaign for free school meals in the UK highlighted child poverty issues and led to important changes in government policies. He's smashing it!

He credits the strength of his faith to his greatest role model in life: his mum. It was her strong faith that helped him find his own. He lives out his purpose to love God and love others by using football as a tool for transformation. And of course, he scores loads of goals along the way!

Sometimes on the road to becoming the person we are meant to be, there are role models that God gives us as examples who springboard us into our future. As we watch their life, it points us to Jesus. For Marcus, it was his mum, but who is that person for you?

We are naturally influenced by those around us. Have you ever been hanging out and chatting away with your friends when suddenly someone suggests ordering pizza? Initially, no one seems interested, but then another friend jumps in, expressing how much they love pizza and how awesome it would be to have some right now. Before you know it, everyone is on board, placing their orders. It becomes a pizza party!

One person's enthusiasm led to a change of behaviour in the whole group. That's peer influence or peer pressure in action. While it's fine for food-related decisions, hanging around people who influence you to make more long-lasting or negative choices can often lead to trouble. Peer pressure is that powerful.

> Do not be misled: 'Bad company corrupts good character.' (1 Corinthians 15:33)

Pastor Craig Groeschel once said, 'Show me your friends, and I'll show you your future. The people you're hanging out with today are shaping the person you will become tomorrow.'[3] This is a great reminder we need to be so careful with choosing our mates. And it's why being part of a church community is vital to help us connect with those who are also seeking to be influenced by Christ.

HIGHLIGHT REEL: DAVID'S BEST FRIEND

David and Jonathan's friendship is a great example of how positive influences in our lives can point us towards God's plans rather than away from them. The story kicks in around 1 Samuel 18. Jonathan, the son of King Saul, was next in line to the throne, but he recognised that God had chosen David instead. Rather than being jealous and trying to compete, Jonathan became David's best friend. He knew that God's plan was best.

When King Saul got jealous and tried to kill David, Jonathan had his back. He warned David, stood up to his dad, and even risked his life to keep David safe. Jonathan encouraged David to trust God, reminding him not to be afraid because God had a plan for him, even when things seemed to be going wrong. This encouraged him to keep going.

Jonathan's influence on David was huge – he was the kind of friend who made David stronger in his faith and helped him stay on the right path. They probably shared common interests like archery, exploring the wilderness, music, and storytelling. But more importantly, their friendship was built on loyalty, trust, and putting God first. Even after Jonathan died in a big battle, David stayed loyal by taking care of Jonathan's family.

Jonathan's willingness to support David, often at his own expense, reflects true selflessness and humility. The good news we have is that Christ is the ultimate friend who made the ultimate sacrifice for us. This is why Jesus is the one who always points us to our God-given purpose.

INFLUENCED BY CULTURE

It is not just *who* but *what* you allow to influence you, that has the power to shape your life. Everything from our background, education, and even our nationality informs our beliefs and behaviour. It's often challenging to discern which voice to go with, especially when they conflict with each other.

It gets even more difficult when considering the influence of the media. We're shown a prescriptive vision of how we should live. The change in our thinking often starts slowly, like a drip, then it becomes a trickle, until it becomes a rushing river that leaves a mark as deep as the Grand Canyon.

For example, if you're always tuning in to podcasts or scrolling YouTube videos on getting those perfect muscles or that perfect shape, it's natural to feel motivated to hit the gym. And hey, that's not a bad thing at all. But take that too far and you start to put your value in how much stronger or fitter you are than others. It might even redefine your idea of what it means to be a real man or real woman. Sometimes it's worth taking a step back and questioning your influences to see if they are healthy for you.

Every day, we're bombarded with messages like:

- 'Buy this product and you will be truly happy…'

- 'Wear this symbol and you will be part of the IN crowd...'
- 'Live this lifestyle and you will be free...'

Most of these messages are from people who just want our money, time, and attention. They're not really looking out for us. Even if we buy what they're selling, it rarely makes us as happy as they promised. Yet we still find ourselves under their influence!

We might not think watching movies or bingeing shows affect us much, but the characters' stories and choices shape our views more than we know. We might slowly start wanting a flashy Hollywood life, all about lots of sex, money, and power. But check the news; it usually leads to a dead end! God's word shows us a better way.

> Your word is a lamp for my feet, a light on my path. (Psalm 119:105)

It's important to ask: 'What does this show, podcast, book, or movie teach me compared to what Jesus says about who I am and my purpose?' We need to learn to discern and filter what we listen to and watch, in line with what the Bible teaches us.

Imagine you're lost in the woods in the pitch black with no idea which way to turn next. You have no torch, map, or compass to guide you. It's getting colder by the minute, and you're worried you will never find your way out.

Suddenly you see a tiny prick of light in the sky – it's the North Star. While other stars move around, this star always shows us where north is. It's a handy guide for figuring out directions and gives you a clear reference point to navigate your way through the darkness.

In the Old Testament, the Israelites (God's people) were captured and held in a foreign land called Babylon far away from home. They had been close to God in the past but now they were feeling uncertain and hopeless about their future. They had lost their North Star.

This meant they listened to whichever voice made the loudest noise or the one that promised to get them through. Babylon was a culture just like today, where everyone was trying to influence and tell others what to do. Some people were even claiming to speak on behalf of God but secretly they had their own agenda.

These local influencers would say things like:

- 'We have plans for you…'
- 'We can offer you a future…'
- 'This thing will give you hope…'

But God spoke through one of his real prophets (those who bring God's message). Jeremiah reassures them:

> 'For I know the plans I have for you,' declares the LORD, 'plans to prosper you and not to harm you, plans to give you hope and a future.' (Jeremiah 29:11)

God spoke in the middle of the lies and confusion to bring clarity of purpose. In a world where we could easily be distracted by so many different voices around us that can't be trusted, there is still one voice that says to you and me:

'Hey…
I know you…
I know the plans that I have for you…
And they are very good plans….
Listen to me…'

God knew we would need more than just a positive message to shape our lives. We need to know we're loved and belong. Then once we're part of God's family, we need someone to show us what that looks like. We need an example to follow. And this is where Jesus becomes our North Star.

INFLUENCED BY JESUS

Back in the day, if you followed Jesus, you were called his 'disciple' (it's easier to pronounce than 'Miqaliens' I guess). This word basically means follower, learner, or apprentice. In the time of Jesus, you could choose to follow someone influential and become their disciple.

They would teach you what to think, how to behave, and what to say until you became more like them. This process was called 'being discipled'. All of us follow something. Jesus invited people to follow him.

> 'Come, follow me,' Jesus said...
> (Matthew 4:19)

This starts with allowing Jesus to influence you to think, act, and speak more like him.

As the Bible puts it:

> Follow God's example, therefore, as dearly loved children and walk in the way of love, just as Christ loved us and gave himself up for us as a fragrant offering and sacrifice to God. (Ephesians 5:1–2)

Straight away, the Bible focuses us on who should be our primary influence. We're instructed to copy Christ's example in the way he made God his priority and loved others. Rather than just mindlessly doing what our mates tell us to do, or running after an AI robot guide, God gives us a better way with Jesus. Your purpose is to love God and love others, and there is no greater example of this than Jesus.

Think about how Jesus is different from the average social influencer. First, Jesus is not there just to offer 'life hacks' to help you solve your problems or achieve your personal goals. What if the goals you want may not be the ones you need? What if God has a better plan for you? You must be willing to respond.

Second, Jesus is not customisable. Jesus is not some sort of Mr. Potato Head that we can mix and match until we are happy with the way he looks (or the way he makes us look). You don't get to pick what you like about him and then edit out or ignore the bits you don't. Instead, we choose to follow Jesus no matter where he leads us. This may mean that we need to make some changes to stay on track.

One of the biggest challenges with online influencers is that no matter how connected you feel to them, they will never really know you, and you can never really know them. They are notoriously difficult to rely on in times of trouble. I mean you don't get to call Ed Sheeran when you break a guitar string do you? Nor do you have a hotline to Taylor Swift when your heart gets broken.

When you are in the thick of it, you don't need an Instagram post to look at or even a celebrity's principles to follow; you need a person to call. You need someone who knows you and loves you completely.

If we want to stay on track with our purpose, we need to learn to depend on Jesus not just try and live how he did. Staying connected with Jesus brings us comfort when we feel overwhelmed trying to figure out God's plan for our lives. Just remember, it's easier to face the future when you aren't trying to prove yourself or make God love you. You belong to him! It then becomes easier to know what to do next when you think about what Jesus did – he loved and served the world around him. If you ever feel stuck, try that first.

Following Jesus' example also helps us avoid the trap of becoming overconfident, assuming we can handle everything on our own. You might look at the life of Jesus and think, 'How on earth can I live like that?' Jesus was filled with the Holy Spirit and totally dependent upon his Father. The good news is that you don't have to do this in your own strength! When we trust him as our source of strength, we shift from 'I've got this!' to 'God's got this.'

Remember, Jesus is not just a figure from history; he is still alive today and willing to help you right now. This is such good news. Jesus doesn't just ask us to follow him but promises to be with us every step of the way. And with Jesus by our side, we can end up being an incredible influence on those around us.

You were made to follow Jesus.

QUESTIONS TO THINK ABOUT:
WHO OR WHAT INFLUENCES ME MOST?

- What are your main influences right now, and are they positive or negative?
- How does culture shape your thinking about yourself and your purpose?
- How can you let Jesus influence more of your life?

T TALENTS | H HOPES | I INFLUENCES | N NEGATIVES | G GROWTH

CHAPTER 5

NEGATIVES

WHAT CHALLENGES DO I NEED TO OVERCOME?

YOU WERE MADE TO OVERCOME.

When Nick Vujicic (pronounced voo-yi-chich) was born without any arms and legs, it was a huge shock to his parents who refused to see or hold him until they were able to deal with their initial grief. This was just the start of the challenges Nick faced every single day growing up in Australia.

Even basic chores were a problem for Nick, such as how to brush your teeth when you can't hold a toothbrush. School bullies were often cruel, which led to feelings of loneliness and depression. He wondered about the meaning of life and whether he had a purpose at all.

Nick's turning point came when he realised that his worth wasn't defined by his physical limitations but by his attitude and newfound faith in Jesus. He figured out how to use a tiny part of his limb he calls his 'chicken drumstick' to perform basic tasks. Now he can type slightly faster than the average person, has learnt how to swim, plays football, and he is even a keen golfer. All without any arms or legs!

Nick grew up to become a motivational speaker and role model, travelling the world to share his story everywhere from schools to prisons, inspiring others to find their purpose. He talks in person and online to millions about his faith in Jesus and how to turn your obstacles into opportunities. He has a loving wife and four children as well as a sense of purpose that changed everything.

As a result of his mission, his website says over 733 million people have heard the good news about Jesus in 60 countries and over a million are now following Christ. Nick found his purpose by helping others find theirs. As he once said:

> 'If God can use a man without arms and legs to be His hands and feet, then He will certainly use any willing heart!'[4]

Nick knew how easy it was to get lost in our own problems, especially when things get tough. But if we want to truly live out our purpose, our focus needs to shift from just our own blocked goals to God's bigger plan. When we align with his vision, everything we do and everything we are starts to make sense. Our lives fit into something much larger than ourselves. Without that focus, we risk getting stuck, locked into our own struggles and missing out on the bigger picture. Nick figured out how to 'love God' and 'love others', no matter what obstacles stood in his way.

PREPARE FOR THE LONG HAUL

We're all about speed these days, right? We are so used to fast food and instant messaging. Plus, ads and social media make it seem like everything should happen instantly. We want results ASAP because waiting feels like forever. Yet the Bible is clear that we need to hang on in there and stick with it if we are going to live in line with God's plan for our lives. We can't give up at the first hurdle.

> You need to persevere so that when you have done the will of God, you will receive what he has promised. (Hebrews 10:36)

In this chapter we will discover how living in line with God's purpose can be tough at times, but you can make it through in God's strength. It helps to be prepared though!

Some things are worth prepping for. Whereas packing for a short journey is about keeping it light and bringing only the essentials, packing for a longer trip requires a different strategy. You'll need to consider the weather conditions and think about every possible scenario. Packing smartly is vital to make sure you are not left short. This is the kind of thinking you need to adopt when planning for a purposeful life.

We need to prepare for distractions, prepare for the unexpected, prepare our emotions, and even prepare to be criticised.

PREPARE FOR DISTRACTIONS

Keep focused on Jesus to avoid going off track.

One of the best Escape Rooms in the world is apparently The Vault in Amsterdam, Netherlands. It's based inside a real bank vault, meaning it feels like you're stepping onto a movie set when you show up for a game. Once inside, you have 80 minutes to break in and retrieve a mysterious item. You contend with green lasers, large blueprints, and even real-life bank guards as part of the game. It's supposed to be a thrilling, puzzling challenge full of excitement and intrigue!

Imagine going into that Escape Room and instead of focusing on the mission, you sit back, scroll on your phone, read a magazine, or chill with a coffee. Then, at the last minute, you realise you are supposed to be solving a puzzle before the clock runs out. That method is doomed for failure, yet many people take this approach in life!

To beat any Escape Room, you need to stay focused and avoid getting diverted. Who you have with you is important too. Some teammates will work well with you and unlock helpful clues, pointing you in the right direction. They're the ones you want to listen to. But then there are others who bring their own agenda, a lot of pointless drama, or try to make it all about them rather than the mission.

It's the same in life. If you are too busy being distracted, or being dragged around by others' agendas, then you might find that the clock runs out. Figure out which voices to listen to and who's going to be on your team if you want to make it through.

But it's not just people. There's a whole world of distraction out there – sports, hobbies, fashion, and endless studies – all of which can make us lose focus. How do you avoid distractions? Fix your eyes on Jesus. He is like a guide in an Escape Room, helping you stay focused on the mission and leading you through every challenge. Keep learning about him, praying to him, and seeking to become more like him.

> ... let us throw off everything that hinders and the sin that so easily entangles. And let us run with perseverance the race marked

> out for us, fixing our eyes on Jesus, the pioneer and perfecter of faith. (Hebrews 12:1–2)

One of the best ways to stay focused is to build habits that put God first. Try turning up to church or youth group regularly – it's a great way to reset and refocus on what really matters. You can also start your day by reading a couple of Bible verses before checking your phone. It's not about following more rules, but about finding little moments that help you stay connected to God. These small changes will help you stay grounded and keep your faith strong.

PREPARE FOR THE UNEXPECTED

Your purpose is not defined by your setbacks.

Bethany Hamilton was a 13-year-old teenager from Hawaii with a bright future ahead of her as a rising surf star. She lived by the beach and competing in surf competitions was her thing. One day she went surfing with her best mate and was randomly attacked by a 14-foot-long tiger shark. It bit off Bethany's left arm, which was dangling in the water, just below the shoulder.

However, not long after the attack, Bethany was back surfing again with only one arm, and within two years had won a national surfing title. Her purpose was to live for Jesus and make a difference by being a role model for others. She went on to become a professional surfer and credits the source of her come-back to her faith in God.

Sometimes life can bite us like a 14-foot shark! You've got a solid plan, and then boom – something totally unexpected happens and knocks you off course.

How do you prepare for the unexpected? When bad things happen people may react with shock, sadness, anger, and fear. Bethany found her way through this with God:

> 'God will give us the strength to be able to handle things. I mean, you can try to do it on your own, and sometimes you can pull off some stuff, but in the long run, it's much easier with him by our side.'[5]

It would have been so easy to blame God, or give up, but instead Bethany overcame by drawing on

God's strength not her own. Our plans may change but God's purpose for the world doesn't, and in every circumstance we have opportunity to love and serve others. This is a fantastic lesson for us all.

If your purpose is only seen as something tied to just one event, achievement, or role, it can leave you feeling stuck or lost when that thing changes. But if we recognise that our purpose is bigger than any one circumstance, it becomes a constant thread running through everything we do.

PREPARE YOUR EMOTIONS

Your purpose is not defined by how you feel in a moment.

Steel Vengeance in Cedar Point theme park in the USA is known for its record-breaking height and speed. It is the tallest (205 feet) and fastest (74 mph) hybrid coaster in the world. It features four inversions, including a 200-foot-tall vertical loop and a 'Twisted Snake Dive', which kind of sounds like it would make you vomit and laugh at the same time.

Life can feel like that rollercoaster sometimes, full of ups and downs happening all at once. Just like emojis in a group chat, we might experience moments of laughter, tears, excitement, or even confusion. All on the same day!

It is vital not to let the rollercoaster of our emotions determine how we respond to what God is asking us to do. Sometimes good and bad stuff can happen at the same time. That's part of life. It doesn't mean that you are getting it wrong, it just means you are human. Keep moving forward.

> 'Success is not final, failure is not fatal:
> It is the courage to continue that counts.'[6]

So, how do you keep moving forward? Don't let problems cling to you like glue. One bad day doesn't equal a bad life! Your feelings are real, and they matter, but remember, they – and your circumstances – can change. Acknowledge your emotions, but don't let them take control of your life.

There is one emotion you can focus on that can help you prepare for any challenge: joy. Happiness is like a quick burst of satisfaction from something fun or exciting happening around you. Joy is that deep feeling of peace and contentment, regardless of our circumstances, because we know that God is good. Joy sticks around longer, while happiness can come and go.

God reminds us to choose joy on the inside even when it's hard on the outside.

> We can rejoice, too, when we run into problems and trials, for we know that they help us develop endurance. And endurance develops strength of character, and character strengthens our confident hope of salvation. And this hope will not lead to disappointment. (Romans 5:3–5, NLT)

How can I be joyful when things are hard? It is not about faking it but framing it. Remember that all bad stuff ends, and God can turn any situation around. Choosing joy is like that rollercoaster strap bar that keeps you locked into your purpose when life seems full of twists and turns. That's how you prepare yourself.

PREPARE TO BE CRITICISED

Your purpose is not determined by what others think but by what God says.

Heidi Crowter is a British disability rights campaigner who has been active in advocating for the rights of people with Down's syndrome. Heidi is a Christian with Down's syndrome herself and she is known for her outspoken stance on promoting dignity and equality, often using her platform to challenge stereotypes and encourage positive change. Yet rather than always being applauded for doing this, she has received a load of online hate. It's crazy to think that even someone whose focus is to do such good can be criticised by others.

Sometimes criticism can be fair, and constructive feedback can help us grow, but when it becomes personal and insulting, it can make us want to give up, throw in the towel, and stop seeking to love others. That's when we have to remind ourselves we are living for God, not people.

As you start to understand who you are and begin to make choices in line with what you are called to do, one thing is for sure: you will stand out from other people. You won't fit in anymore with the crowd. Most people go with the flow. When you live differently, some might not understand you, they may pressure you to conform, and they might even get mad at you for being different. Keep going anyway. It's like Paul says in the Bible:

> Am I now trying to win the approval of human beings, or of God? Or am I trying to please people? If I were still trying to please people, I would not be a servant of Christ. (Galatians 1:10)

In a world where people can be quick to judge, remember that you belong to God. Keep following your path, even if it means standing out. Ultimately, it's not about pleasing everyone – it's about staying true to Jesus above all else.

KEEP GOING

Living purposefully is not a one-off moment or event.

We often watch movies that build up to a big, dramatic climax – the hero finally saves the day or achieves their dream all in the last fifteen minutes.

It's easy to think that fulfilling your purpose is about waiting for that huge, one-time event. But in real life, it's more about what goes on behind the scenes. It's about the everyday choices you make to love others, the small steps you take to make a difference to those around you, the consistent effort to put Jesus first. The truth is, it's our small daily decisions that shape our impact.

HIGHLIGHT REEL: DAVID'S BATTLES

As a young man, one of the biggest challenges David had to overcome was a literal giant named Goliath. It's a fab story you can read in 1 Samuel 17.

The Philistines were waging war against God's people the Israelites. The Philistines' champion, Goliath, has been shouting backwards and forwards to the Israelite army insulting them and challenging anyone who's brave enough to come out for a scrap. David is too young to be a soldier; he's only there delivering supplies to his older brothers, but in the absence of anyone else being willing to fight, he steps up.

David says to King Saul something like, 'As a shepherd, I protected my father's sheep from lions and bears. I defeated them to save the flock. Just as God helped me then, he will help me defeat this bad guy once and for all.'

Then David, just a young shepherd boy, defeats the giant warrior Goliath with a single stone shot from a sling.

But if you look closely at the story, this 'one-off' victory was not actually out of the ordinary for David. He had trained by having lots of little battles with lions and bears out in the field that no one else knew about. His faith was shaped as he experienced God deliver him again and again. As he says:

> The Lord who rescued me from the paw of the lion and the paw of the bear will rescue me from the hand of this Philistine. (1 Samuel 17:37)

Now, it's probably not a great idea to tell you to go around scrapping with wild animals to practise your fighting skills. That would likely end up on someone's TikTok feed. The key thing is that we trust God in the little things before the big thing comes our way.

The 'little lions and bears' in our lives can represent the everyday challenges, obstacles, or responsibilities, that we overcome in God's strength before facing more daunting stuff. It was what David did in private that made a difference in public.

David's victory over Goliath might teach us that facing smaller challenges prepares us for bigger ones. But the real hero of our story is Jesus not us. Christ is the one who conquered the ultimate challenge – making us right with God again – through his sacrifice on the cross. Just like David, Jesus stepped out alone and faced a big fight and ultimately won the biggest victory of all. This means that with Jesus, we never have to fight our battles alone.

Jesus' teaching reminds us that even the smallest actions matter and can lead to something much greater. So, don't underestimate the power of your everyday choices – they're laying the groundwork for the future you're building.

> Whoever can be trusted with very little can also be trusted with much... (Luke 16:10)

Sure, you might do something big for God in the future that others will notice, but for now, focus on what's in front of you. This helps you find purpose even in the hard stuff of life.

You were made to overcome.

QUESTIONS TO THINK ABOUT: WHAT CHALLENGES DO I NEED TO OVERCOME?

- Which of these – distractions, unexpected events, emotional ups and downs, or criticism from others – are the biggest barriers you're facing right now?
- What was one recent challenge you've overcome, and how did you beat it?
- How might relying on God's strength help you tackle your next problem?

CHAPTER 6

GROWTH

HOW DO I GROW IN MY PURPOSE?

YOU WERE MADE TO BE CONNECTED TO GOD.

Peter Glazebrook is an amateur gardener who lives in the heart of England and his unusual dream is to grow the biggest veggies the world has ever seen. One day he decided to go all in and join the National Giant Vegetables Championship – yep, that's a real thing! The rules? Super strict. And the competition? Fierce. But Peter was ready.

For a whole year, Peter focused on nurturing his veggies, aiming to make them giant-sized. He fed them the right stuff and kept the soil super healthy. It worked a treat. He eventually racked up several Guinness World Records for his monster produce. One of his potatoes weighed a whopping 4.98 kilograms – that's like the weight of eight basketballs! Can you imagine the mountain of chips you could make from that one spud?

But that's nothing compared to other heavyweight champions that came from the same competition: the world's heaviest green marrow tipped the scales at a jaw-dropping 116.4 kilograms. That's as heavy as a giant panda or a baby elephant!

Apparently, the secret to growing vegetables that break records is to feed them a healthy mix of nutrients and create the right kind of fertiliser for the soil. Similarly, the Bible has a lot to say about creating a healthy environment where we can grow in our faith.

In this chapter we will discover the key to creating a purposeful life that produces results. Personal growth happens when we stay connected to Jesus.

> I am the vine; you are the branches. If you remain in me and I in you, you will bear

> much fruit; apart from me you can do nothing. (John 15:5)

Jesus compared himself to a vine and his followers to branches. Just as a vine needs to nourish the branches for them to grow, we also need to stay connected to Jesus and be dependent on him. When we talk about 'fruit' here we aren't talking about literal grapes or apples; it's the lasting results that come from saying yes to Jesus. Impact comes when we do what God asks us to do. Many people think of results or success as gaining more fame, fortune, and power. This is not the way of Jesus.

Christian fruit is shown through actions like helping the poor, visiting the sick, supporting friends and family, doing acts of kindness, sharing your faith, volunteering, standing up for justice, being honest, encouraging others, and forgiving those who have wronged you. These deeds are the fruit of God's love and Jesus' teachings in your life.

The opposite of being fruitful is doing our own thing; relying on our own strength to make a difference. Without God's guidance and strength, our efforts may not lead to lasting change. With so many needs in the world, it's easy to end up feeling overwhelmed. On our own, we might help temporarily, but the world often ends up just as troubled as before. But with God, things can change forever.

Another danger is that we might begin to take credit when good things start happening and we think we're all that! Pride can creep in, making us focus on ourselves instead of on God. This misses the whole point. Without our connection with God, our efforts are fruitless. Staying close to God is the key. He's our true source of power.

Living a life of purpose means you will produce long-lasting results for God. Jesus makes this as visible as a giant vegetable when he says:

> You did not choose me, but I chose you and appointed you so that you might go and bear fruit – fruit that will last... (John 15:16)

There is a reminder here that we don't control the results; God does. If God is using you to produce lots of bananas that's great because that's needed right now! There's no point in wishing God was making pineapples through you instead! Don't worry about comparing yourself to your friends or people you see online and thinking, 'I wish my life and impact were more like that!' Instead, focus on loving and serving others to keep living out your purpose right where you are.

So how can we remain connected to Jesus and be fruitful in all we do? It starts by saying **yes** to God, saying **please** in prayer, saying **sorry** for mistakes, and saying **thank you** for blessings.

SAY YES MORE

A man named Danny Wallace once tried an experiment where he committed to saying 'yes' to every opportunity that came his way. This was inspired by a stranger who advised him to 'say yes more' after he felt like his life was going downhill following a breakup with his girlfriend.

As a result of saying yes, some incredible things happened to Danny, including winning $45,000, becoming a television executive, travelling the globe, and even reportedly meeting a magical dog wearing a hat! There is great power in saying yes!

As Christians, we don't just say yes to random things; we say yes to Jesus. In fact, that is the essence of what it means to be a follower of Christ. Saying 'yes' to Jesus every day involves living out your faith and committing to follow him in your daily life.

One of the ways we can figure out how to do this is by reading more about Jesus in the Bible. Start with Matthew, Mark, Luke, and John – these 'Gospels' (good news stories) show us who Jesus is and why his life and teachings matter. When we read about Jesus, it gives us insight into how we might say yes to him.

Jesus taught us some powerful lessons that we can put into practice every day. He said to treat others the way you want to be treated, and even love your enemies and pray for those who hurt you. He challenged us to forgive people just as God forgives us and to serve others without expecting anything in return.

These are just nice ideas until we do something about them.

> Therefore everyone who hears these words of mine and puts them into practice is like a wise man who built his house on the rock. (Matthew 7:24)

As you read the Bible, you have to put what you've learnt into practice, or nothing will really change in your life. Jesus' teaching goes beyond the classroom. He offers more than pointless facts you'll never use again; Christ offers real-life learning rooted in relationship – this is not just a religious lesson, but an invitation to adventure.

Living for Jesus means choosing to centre your life around his teachings and example to love God and others. Without him, life can feel as confusing as trying to assemble a Lego set without the box or instructions – just a pile of bricks with no clear idea of what you're meant to build. In Christ, though, we find out who we are and what we're living for. It's like suddenly seeing the front of the Lego box: you see the bigger picture of your life, understand the design, and know how the pieces fit together. Following Jesus is like having the instruction manual, guiding you to live out your true purpose.

Saying yes to Jesus is like fertiliser; it helps you grow.

SAY PLEASE MORE

Prayer simply means talking to God in a natural way. Some people think prayer is that thing that you do before mealtimes or once a week on a Sunday, but it's way more important than that.

Prayer is *not* about:

- Chanting and babbling repeated phrases in the hope of getting God's attention.
- Acting like God is a genie in a lamp who will grant your every wish.
- Trying to twist God's arm to give you whatever you want.
- Being clever enough or loud enough to impress God.
- Knowing enough or being good enough before you can start.

Prayer helps us plug into our source. When you pray you often feel God's comforting, guiding presence with you like a supportive friend. But even if you don't feel anything, you can be confident that God hears you.

- Ask for everything you need – practical, emotional, relational, and spiritual. A good Father wants to provide for his children.
- Seek wisdom when you find yourself in a crisis or an impossible situation.
- Share your worries, anxieties, and fears with God because he cares deeply for you.
- Pray for others in need, including church and national leaders, and for global issues like war and famine.

George Müller was a famous Christian missionary and orphanage founder in the 19th century. He lived for Jesus and made a difference to others by serving the poor. Despite having no real wealth to run his orphanages, Müller trusted in God's provision every single day. He regularly prayed and miraculously, time and again, donations of food, money, and resources would arrive just when they were needed most.

> The prayer of a righteous person is powerful and effective. (James 5:16)

One time, when the children at the orphanage had no food for breakfast, Müller gathered everyone to pray. While they were praying, there was a knock at the door. A baker stood there, saying he hadn't been able to sleep and felt he should bake bread for them. Then, a milkman showed up because his cart had broken down nearby, and he gave them milk to prevent it from going off. God answered their prayers right away.

Prayer is that powerful! You won't stay connected to Jesus without it.

Prayer is like fertiliser; it helps you grow.

SAY SORRY MORE

The word 'sin' means doing wrong or missing the mark. All of us mess up in big and small ways all the time. Only Jesus has a perfect track record. There are many things that get in the way of our relationship with God. These include lying, cheating, or doing things that hurt yourself or someone else. Sin is more than just actions though. We sin when we put anything in the top spot of our lives rather than God. What happens when we fall short? We have to go to God and say that we are sorry. That's the only way to get cleaned up. We need a rescuer. We can't work our way out of it or just ignore it and pretend it never happened.

> But if we confess our sins to him, he is faithful and just to forgive us our sins and to cleanse us from all wickedness. (1 John 1:9, NLT)

Did you ever get in trouble at school and experience sweaty palms and nervousness when being sent to the headteacher's office? Some headteachers have a reputation for being strict and stern, spreading fear among those who interact with them. They rule with an iron fist! Some people worry approaching God feels a bit like this.

It can be hard to accept what those in authority tell us to do, especially if we don't trust that they know us, value us, or have our best interests at heart. What if God's like this?

The writer A.W. Tozer said, 'What comes into our minds when we think about God is the most important thing about us.'[7] What a tragedy if we start to see God like that strict headteacher or someone who's just telling us what to do without caring about us! The Bible says we can always come to God assured of a warm welcome even when we get it wrong.

> Because of Christ and our faith in him, we can now come boldly and confidently into God's presence. (Ephesians 3:12, NLT)

If Jesus ran your school, there would always be a 'second chance' policy for the students. Whenever we remind God of our mistakes, he will always remind us we were made to belong to him.

> ***God's forgiveness is like fertiliser; it helps you grow.***

HIGHLIGHT REEL: DAVID'S HUGE MISTAKE

David, now the King of Israel, was known for being a mighty warrior and leader, but he didn't always get it right. Sometimes he got it horrendously wrong. Once he had an affair with a woman called Bathsheba, who was married to one of his soldiers. Bathsheba became pregnant and David later tried to cover up his actions by arranging for her husband to be killed in battle. It was a complete mess. His sin included lies, deceit, and even ended in murder. You can read the sad story in 2 Samuel 11.

Eventually, David turned to God to ask for forgiveness and deal with the problems he had caused. He was deeply distressed about how much he had hurt people, fearing that his sin would block him from ever being part of God's purposes again. This is what he wrote in one of his psalms during that time:

> Have mercy on me, O God, because of your unfailing love. Because of your great compassion, blot out the stain of my sins. (Psalm 51:1, NLT)

God was faithful and showed mercy to David, despite the serious consequences of his actions. David had to learn to receive God's forgiveness and rediscover his purpose. The good news for us is that Jesus offers us unconditional forgiveness and grace, no matter how big our mess-ups or wrongdoing. Through Jesus, we can receive God's mercy, find a fresh start, and get back on track with God's purposes of loving and serving, just as David did.

SAY THANK YOU MORE

Gratitude is being thankful for what we have. It's about recognising the good in your life and feeling appreciative. Here's what the Bible says the result of growing in God looks like:

> So then, just as you received Christ Jesus as Lord, continue to live your lives in him, rooted and built up in him, strengthened in the faith as you were taught, and overflowing with thankfulness. (Colossians 2:6–7)

There are five stages of growth in this verse:

1. **Receive Jesus**: Decide to accept Jesus Christ as the boss of your life. Say yes to Jesus and your life will never be the same again.

2. **Live your life with Jesus**: Involve Jesus in every aspect of your life. Let his teachings and example guide your thoughts, words, and actions every day.

3. **Get built up**: Study the Bible and engage in prayer and friendship with other Christians. Keep yourself grounded in God.

4. **Strengthen your faith**: Trust in God's promises and put what you've been taught into action. Do the things you know will help you grow.

5. **Overflow with thankfulness**: Make a habit of gratitude. Regularly express thankfulness to God for all he has done.

When you are a kid, you tend to see the world with awe and wonder and are enthusiastic for every little thing. Yet when we get older, we often let the negatives and the stuff we want (but don't have) cloud our view. In God's eyes, experiencing wonder and remaining grateful are signs of maturity and 'growing up'.

Gratitude is like fertiliser; it helps you grow.

GROW MORE LIKE JESUS

You might think that working out God's plan for your life is some exact standard that you can never quite live up to. How can you tell if you're even on the right track? It's not like God marks your homework at the end of every week and then gives you back the results. Perhaps a simple way to check if you're heading in the right direction is to ask yourself this question regularly: Am I becoming more like Jesus or less?

There are so many positive qualities you will see if you're growing more like Jesus. As the Bible says:

> The fruit of the Spirit is love, joy, peace, patience, kindness, goodness, faithfulness, gentleness and self-control. (Galatians 5:22–23, ESV)

What then might this look like in your life? Here are some questions to reflect on for each characteristic.

- **Love**: Am I showing kindness to everyone around me and letting go of grudges?
- **Joy**: Am I being content rather than always longing for what I don't have?
- **Peace**: Am I staying calm and helping others find peace in difficult situations?
- **Patience**: Am I waiting calmly for the things I want or need without getting impatient or upset?
- **Kindness**: Am I doing kind things for others without expecting anything in return?

- **Goodness**: Am I consistently choosing to do the right thing, even when it's hard?
- **Faithfulness**: Am I being loyal and keeping the promises I make to others?
- **Gentleness**: Am I approaching others with care in both my actions and words?
- **Self-control**: Am I managing my emotions and actions effectively, especially in challenging situations?

Imagine a sculptor creating a statue of a horse from a block of marble. The sculptor carefully chips away every piece of marble that doesn't look like a horse, revealing the beautiful form within. Similarly, in our lives, God works like the sculptor, helping us remove everything that doesn't align with who we are meant to be.

This process is fuelled by the power of God: The Holy Spirit. When you believe in Jesus, the Holy Spirit comes into your life to guide you, give you strength, and help you stay on track.

Think of it like this: just like you need to charge your phone to keep it going, we need the Holy Spirit to empower us to live more like Jesus. The

Holy Spirit is your constant connection to God. He's there to help you love people better, be patient, and keep hope even when life gets tough.

God wants you to be shaped by Jesus until you become more like him: loving God and loving others.

The ultimate fruit we can ever bear is to live a life of love, patience, kindness, and goodness – just like Jesus. By staying close to God, you can stay close to your purpose.

You were made to be connected to God.

QUESTIONS TO THINK ABOUT: HOW DO I GROW IN MY PURPOSE?

- What are you doing to grow in your relationship with God right now?
- Which of these areas – expressing gratitude, seeking forgiveness, or saying yes to God – do you think you need to focus on this week?
- What does the idea of becoming more like Jesus mean to you?

OUTRO

I was today years old when I found out that sea turtles have a form of Wi-Fi in their heads. Bet you didn't expect to read that sentence today! Instead of logging on to catch up on the latest cat videos, turtles use a tiny receptor that doesn't connect to the internet but links directly to the earth's magnetic waves. What does this little button in their brains allow them to do? It is like a built-in compass helping them find their way back to the place they were born, no matter where they are in the world.

One such sea turtle named Yoshi was tracked from Australia to the waters of Angola on Africa's eastern coast and back, a record trip of 22,000 miles! After a long journey the turtle reached the spot where she once hatched as a baby. She dug a hole in the sand and laid her eggs securing the future generations before returning to the sea. Mission accomplished.

It may not be every day that you feel jealous of a sea turtle, but it must be amazing to have such a clear goal, right? Well would you be 'shell shocked' to know that it is possible to get as clear about your purpose as Yoshi the leatherback turtle?

As you wrap up this book, remember the heart of the message: you find your purpose as you get on board with God's purposes for you and for the world, even if your personal path isn't crystal clear every single day. Instead of stressing about finding the perfect direction, focus on joining in with what God is already doing around you. Embrace opportunities to love God and others right where you are – whether it's at home, at church, at school, or in your community. It's about prioritising God's purposes over our own agendas.

You will never go far wrong when you focus on loving God and serving others.

Consider that it's not a coincidence that you're in your current situation. Nobody else can reach your family and friends in the same way as you. God has put you there intentionally as part of his plan. Jump into whatever God has for you to do today and trust that God is guiding you in every step you take. Never forget you are God's masterpiece. He has prepared good things for you to do:

> For we are God's handiwork, created in Christ Jesus to do good works, which God prepared in advance for us to do. (Ephesians 2:10)

God sent Jesus not just to show us our purpose but to help us live it out. Even when you're tempted to go your own way, keep your eyes on what truly matters and trust that staying on track with God's plan will lead to a more meaningful and satisfying life. Remember:

> It's in Christ that we find out who we are and what we are living for. (Ephesians 1:11, MSG)

By always looking to Jesus, you can discover a sense of self and purpose that aligns with a greater plan, giving you a solid foundation to live your life upon.

A LIFE WORTH LIVING

Picture this scene for a moment: It's your 90th

birthday party and you are about to make a speech in front of all your family and friends. As you start to share, you tell of all the significant moments that have shaped your life. You speak of your most embarrassing mistakes, your scariest experiences, and the wonderful moments that took your breath away. You end by reflecting that your life has flown by in an instant and it seems like only yesterday that you were a teenager, sitting in school, waiting for the bell to ring at the end of another day.

Looking back over life, you'll probably wonder what difference you made in the world.

Imagining this scene may act like a wakeup call. Life is short! We don't talk about it very often but really we all know our time in this world isn't going to last forever.

Every person's record includes their name, the date they were born, and eventually, the date they leave this world.

What we do with the space between the beginning and end of our earthly lives matters.

Imagine being able to look back and see the faithfulness of God in every situation you've encountered. Imagine really loving others the way Jesus loves them.

One day we will all face our creator and if you are a Christian your goal is to hear these words from God:

> Well done, my good and faithful servant. You have been faithful ... Let's celebrate together! (Matthew 25:23, NLT)

That vision is worth giving your whole life for. At the end of your life, you want to be able to say, 'Mission accomplished'.

DO THE NEXT RIGHT THING

Throughout this book we have looked at five questions that any young person can ask themselves to help discover how they can love and serve:

T is for Talents: What are my God-given talents?
H is for Hopes: What do I hope and dream for?
I is for Influences: Who or what influences me most?
N is for Negatives: What challenges do I need to overcome?
G is for Growth: How do I grow in my purpose?

Hopefully you are starting to figure out what truly matters. Discovering God's purpose can be exciting and motivating. When you know your purpose, it's like finding a special path made just for you. It gives you a clear direction and helps you focus on what you really care about.

So, what can you do next? Why not set some G-O-D Goals based on what you've learnt?

G – GET CLARITY

Look back at each chapter again and set some clear goals for yourself. Stay focused.

Ideas might include:

- I want to love God by...
- I want to love others by...
- My top three talents are...
- The thing I hope for the most right now is...
- The influences I want to have in my life are...
- The main barriers I have are...
- The thing I will do to overcome barriers is...

O – OUTLINE STEPS

Break down your goal into manageable steps. Create a roadmap of what actions you need to take next. Stay active.

Ideas might include:

- The first thing I will do is...
- The next step I will take is...
- One person I need to ask for help is...
- A skill I need to develop is...

D – DEVOTE YOURSELF

Make a deeper connection with God through prayer, reflection, and seeking his guidance. Stay close.

Ideas might include:

- What I will pray for next is...
- What I will read in the Bible next is...

- The thing I am most grateful for right now is…
- One thing I need to say sorry for is...
- The thing that is holding me back from following Jesus is…

Take time to develop actionable G-O-D Goals that will help you make progress towards living out your purpose. Remember, none of this can be done in your own strength. You need Jesus every step of the way.

HIGHLIGHT REEL: DAVID'S LEGACY

David went down in history as someone who tried to follow God's purpose for his life despite not always getting it right along the way. In the Bible book of Acts it says this about David at the end of his life:

> Now when David had served God's purpose in his own generation, he fell asleep... (Acts 13:36)

What's interesting is that Acts doesn't say: 'David did his own thing' or 'David followed his heart.'

Instead he sought to follow God's purpose not his own. As you figure out your next steps, it's not just about chasing after what seems exciting or what everyone else is doing. It's about seeking out and following God's purpose for your life.

Like David, you'll find greater fulfilment and direction by focusing on what God has planned for you, rather than just going with the flow or making decisions based solely on your own desires. When you take your eyes off yourself and fix them on Jesus it changes everything.

Right now, you are part of a generation that doesn't have a clue about the things you've just read in this book. Chances are, most of the people around you won't know what you have discovered about Jesus and his purpose for your life. Knowing your purpose is a gift. Don't waste that knowledge! Live it and share it!

What if God could use you like David to serve his purposes in your generation?

ENDNOTES

1 Martay, 'If Billie Eilish's "What Was I Made For?" Was a Christian Song', <https://www.youtube.com/watch?v=-cxb2fZwFlw>

2 'About The Rebelution', <https://www.therebelution.com/about>

3 Craig Groeschel, <https://x.com/craiggroeschel/status/999787468693168129?lang=en>

4 Nick Vujicic, <https://nickvministries.org/about/nick-biography>

5 Bethany Hamilton quoted in Mark Moring, 'A Surfer with Soul', 5 April 2011, *Christianity Today*, <https://www.christianitytoday.com/ct/2011/aprilweb-only/surferwithsoul.html>

6 Quoted by Bear Grylls, 'Bear Grylls on Turning Defeat into Victory' 15 July 2016, GQ, <https://www.gq-magazine.co.uk/article/bear-grylls-on-turning-defeat-into-victory>

7 A.W. Tozer, *The Knowledge of the Holy* (HarperCollins, 1978), p. 1.